IF YOU HAVE TO DO IT,
You Might as Well Get Good at It

A Comprehensive Shopping Guide for Men

BRENDA ANNETTE RIGHTER

Inspiring Voices®
A Service of **Guideposts**

Inspiring Voices books may be ordered through booksellers or by contacting:

Inspiring Voices
1663 Liberty Drive
Bloomington, IN 47403
www.inspiringvoices.com
1-(866) 697-5313

Because of the dynamic nature of the Internet, any web addresses or links contained in
this book may have changed since publication and may no longer be valid. The views
expressed in this work are solely those of the author and do not necessarily reflect the views
of the publisher, and the publisher hereby disclaims any responsibility for them.

ISBN: 978-1-4624-0125-3 (sc)
ISBN: 978-1-4624-0126-0 (e)

Library of Congress Control Number: 2012937517

Printed in the United States of America

Inspiring Voices rev. date: 06/12/2012

To all the men of the world who try,
and to the women who love them!

Contents

Acknowledgments

First, I'd like to acknowledge my wonderful husband, Scott, for encouraging me in this book project from our very first conversation about it. Without him, there would have been no need for this book.

Second, I want to express my eternal gratitude to my mom, Sarah, for always believing in me and encouraging me. Even though she's not a shopper, she is a fabulous mom!

Third in line is Victoria Jacoby for being my accountability partner for many years. She has helped me stay on track with my dreams and goals and has encouraged me to continue moving forward. She also drew the comic strips for the book, which added great flavor and humor to the content.

Other wonderful friends and encouragers include Chet Marshall and Janine Burnett. Their faith in my efforts is so greatly appreciated.

Introduction

One day last December, when my husband, Scott, announced for the umpteenth time that he had absolutely no idea what to get me for Christmas, I just about had the proverbial cow. "Are you kidding me? What do you mean you have no idea? Um, hello ... we've been married for twenty-three years, for goodness sake. You live with me every day. You know what I like! You know what I don't like. You know my hobbies. You know my pants and blouse size. You know what I need. Ugh!" Then I proceeded to ask myself how in the world this amazingly smart man could be in this predicament. Why is it so difficult for him to buy me, the woman he knows and loves, a gift? How can he be so smart and efficient and resourceful and creative during the eleven months leading up to a gift-buying opportunity (birthday, Valentine's Day, Christmas) and then not be able to use all these same wonderful attributes once it becomes obvious that it is time to head out to the stores for some good old-fashioned shopping and gift-buying? How does this happen?

After the smoke cleared and I was able to think clearly again (also known as thirty minutes), I asked him a few questions—questions like how could he not know what to buy me after all these years and how does he not know what I would like as a gift? His response, "I don't know. You are so hard to shop for." And then he gave me that look—you know the one I'm referring to because you've probably given the same look—the look of "please don't make me go shopping.

I'll do almost anything to not have to go shopping." I just rolled my eyes and moved on.

A few days later, I went to lunch with a friend. We'll call her Veronica. I was sharing my enormously tragic situation with Veronica, and you know what she told me? She said her husband said the same thing! What? How can that be? You mean to tell me there are *two* clueless men out there wandering around the mall with not an idea in their heads for gifts for the most special person in their life? Oh my goodness, this is bigger than I thought.

As we sat and shared a meal and the funny stories of our lives, Veronica proceeded to tell me that she'd bought a few things for herself for the upcoming holiday, things that she wanted and needed, things she decided not to ask her husband for. She planned to wrap them and tell her husband that the gifts were from him.

At this point, you are probably chanting, "Woo hoo. That's what I'm talking about. Let her buy her own gifts. It is just easier that way, and I'm off the hook." But I ask you, is this really how you want your most special relationship to go? Wouldn't you feel better knowing you'd put forth extra effort in purchasing a gift for your honey? Receiving a meaningful gift from the man in her life will make her day. It will fill her heart with contentment beyond what you might realize. And, as an added bonus, it will probably get you out of the doghouse for any previous (or future) infractions.

If I promise to help, through this book, will you at least try? Will you either open your mind for the first time or reopen it and go on an adventure with me?

Nearly any activity can be fun—short of a root canal—*if* you choose to make it fun. When going shopping, remember these key things to help create an enjoyable atmosphere:

1. Take a friend. (Look around the mall the next time you are shopping and you'll see pairs of women. They are having fun shopping together.)

2. Take the kids. (For specific reasons. Create a tradition.)

3. Don't take the kids.

4. Treat yourself afterward (lunch, coffee, etc.).

5. Make it a tradition.

6. Remember why you are shopping/who you are shopping for, and cause it to be special and fun!

And remember, the best gifts are those with these three qualities:

1. Let it be thoughtful, meaning that you thought of getting a gift for a special occasion and you were on time.

2. Let it be individual, specific to the receiver.

3. Let it be from your heart—you are buying because you care about the receiver.

What This Book Can Do For You

Potentially, this book can save your relationship. Okay, maybe not, but still … it can give you a greater understanding of your significant other and cause your relationship to go to a deeper level. Yes, all this can happen as a result of successful gift-giving.

Not convinced? Let's compare how you feel when you've done something to the full extent of your capabilities, when you've put your whole effort into an activity. Now think about the times when you have not done this, when you've only half-heartedly completed a task. Can you tell the difference? If you can tell the difference, do you think others can see it also? Do you want your best girl to feel like you've put minimal effort into buying her a gift? How do you think she'll feel when she knows that you ran to the mall at the eleventh hour and picked up something that "will do the job"? In nearly every relationship there is the component of gift-giving. Do you believe this? If the answer is yes, and you have to do it, you might as well get good at it.

So, as we look through the long (and sometimes obvious) list of gift categories, I hope to dispel the mysterious realm of gift-buying and give you suggestions and ideas for your future years of gift-buying opportunities.

To start this process, tap into your imagination and let it grow. This idea of gift-buying and gift-giving is not rocket science. It does not have to be so difficult or frustrating. Through this book, you'll get suggestions and ideas that will engage your creative mind (and yes, we all have some level of creativity). From there, you'll be able to make that idea your own, add or subtract from an idea to create your own flare, and give a remarkable gift to that special someone in your life.

As you'll see throughout this book, I suggest many times that you get to know your person well. You are probably thinking, "Well, duh.

Of course I should know my soul mate." While it might seem like a silly thing to ask, many men do not know the details or preferences of their person. If I asked you what her favorite color is, if she likes skinny jeans or favors low-heeled shoes, would you know the answers? There are lots of ways to accomplish this. You can ask her or you can become a personal private investigator and look for clues by perusing her closet for trends. You can shop with her to see what she is drawn to or you can ask others around her, such as family members or friends, what types of things she likes.

Enlisting the help of others, people who have been a part of her life for a long time, can be a valuable resource. Don't discount the value of any opportunity to find out more detailed information about her that will help you in your future shopping endeavors.

Another suggestion is to see if she has created a list of things she wants to see or do. Check out the list. What is on it? Does she want to see a play? Then take her to the show. Does she want to run a marathon? Then buy her a new pair of running shoes. Does she want to learn a foreign language? Pay for a class for her at the local community college.

It might seem like an overly generic way to look at shopping, but in general, even if your person is difficult to buy for, there are so many options for gift-buying. You just may be unaware of these options, sometimes even unsure of where to start. It is my hope that we can fix that and send you on your merry way to the mall (or the internet) armed with knowledge that will produce a successful outcome for both you and the recipient of your gift.

So let's get started!

Explanation Of Term

Person in this book refers to the significant female in your life. She can be your wife, your girlfriend, or a platonic female friend. It could even mean your mother or your daughter (in some categories). Many times I will just use the term *she* or *her*. In all cases, this means the special lady in your life.

Gift Categories

CLOTHING

Let's start with the obvious: clothes. Most women love getting new clothing items, and at first glance, this might seem like an easy category to consider. But there's more to clothing purchases than meets the eye. Sure, going to a big department store, such as Macy's or Dillard's, can be fruitful, and you'll probably be able to cross something off your list fairly quickly, but give this category more careful thought. It can be your best friend or put you in the doghouse, depending on how you handle the purchase.

What types of clothes does she like? Is she into the latest fad? Does she like the classics? Does she prefer comfort over fashion or fashion at all cost? Does she like prints or solids? Does she choose to layer her outfits? Does she prefer neutral colors in order to create many outfits from just a few pieces of clothing, or bright and flashy colors that create just one outfit?

> "I base my fashion sense on what doesn't itch."
> Gilda Radner

Uh oh, I can sense it … you are starting to panic. *Stop! Don't panic!* You just need to do a bit of homework and all the above questions can be easily answered; I am here to help. When you see her on any given

1

day, what is she wearing? Does she seem to be focused on comfort? Does she make it a point to match everything from head to toe? Is she wearing bright colors or neutrals?

Make a mental note of things that you notice, or better yet, take notes on your smartphone. This can come in handy. You can quickly make note of something special she is wearing or something she's mentioned she wants from a particular store, and save it for later when it is time to purchase a gift.

Most women, especially if they are past the age of twenty-four, have a specific style they like and feel comfortable in. Your job is to pay attention to this style and notice the nuances of it. This will give you a big payoff in the future.

Let's get started with the basics. Below is a list of items to consider that fall into the clothing category. To help minimize confusion, I have broken down the categories into very specific items. For example, the clothing category includes tops, bottoms, and dresses/ suits. Outerwear, athletic wear, and intimate apparel are covered in separate categories, as are shoes. It may seem some of these items are obvious, but I want to cover each item completely, even though you most likely know details of some of them.

TOPS

There is a myriad of options for tops, as you'll see in the list below. Just as you would find a variety of top styles and fabrics in a man's closet, you'll find a variety in a woman's closet as well.

Blouse – usually dressy, something she would wear to the office, to church, or to a nice restaurant. Possible fabrics include silk and polyester. Blouses are not usually made from a cotton fabric.

<u>Shirt</u> – a little more casual than a blouse. The most common fabric for a shirt is cotton. Quite often, something in the shirt category would need ironing after each wash. Keep this in mind if you know your person doesn't like to iron. If ironing is a non-desired activity, don't buy her a clothing item that requires ironing.

My mom loves to iron. It is one of her favorite chores. I'm quite the opposite. I'd rather shovel horse manure than iron and will only do it if forced to. As a result, my closet is full of wrinkled shirts; actually I should say my husband's closet is full of wrinkled shirts. The shirts in the men's department are so nice and look beautiful in the store, and I'm just sure my hubby will like them as much as I do. So I buy one or two, thrilled with my purchase, and bring them home with a smile. He'll wear the shirt once, I wash it, and it never looks the same. From the dryer, it gets hung on a hanger and goes into the section of the closet where I hang all the items that need to be ironed. It is like a black hole. We rarely see that shirt again.

Moral of the story: be sure your person will iron the shirt or else you'll be wasting your money. As a good alternative, most local dry cleaners will launder and iron shirts at affordable rates. (These days, my husband wears a lot of polyester blends.)

<u>Tank</u> – many women like to wear a tank top under their outer top. Some women do this for fashion while others do it for warmth. Tank tops are in most every clothing store since they are in fashion. They come in a variety of colors and styles, but they all have two things in common: they have narrow, spaghetti-type straps and they hug the body. If you are buying a blouse, sweater, or shirt that is vibrant in color or sheer in fabric, purchasing a tank to match is a great gift idea. She'll love that you put the extra thought into creating a special look for her.

Tunic – sometimes made of yarn or other sweater-like fabric; the biggest difference between a tunic and other tops is the length. Tunic denotes long in length, falling below the natural waistline and most always below the booty. They often come belted.

Tunics are a fun addition to a woman's wardrobe. They are currently in fashion and can be very versatile. Obviously, you won't need to purchase a tank to go under the tunic since it is long, but you can pair it with some leggings (covered in the bottoms section) and have a wonderful gift.

Sweater – we all know about sweaters. They are lovely and warm and cozy. Sweaters are a great gift if you live in a cold climate or if your special lady is cold-natured. There are several types of sweaters: ones worn as stand-alone tops and those worn *over* another top, such as a tank, a T-shirt or a blouse.

The second category is referred to as a cardigan. Cardigans sometimes button down the front or have a zipper or other type of closure, which can be left open if desired.

> **"I've always thought of the T-shirt as the alpha and omega of the fashion alphabet."**
> **Giorgio Armani**

T-shirt – a staple in every woman's wardrobe. T-shirts are classic wear, and many women appreciate a nice comfy T-shirt to fall back on. A T-shirt is a lightweight, usually short-sleeved garment. A new type that has exploded on the fashion scene is called a graphic T. They often come adorned with sequins, glitter, and/or gems. Graphic Ts are beautiful and take the classic T a step farther. They can be worn with nearly any casual bottom. One word of warning: some brands of graphic Ts tend to run small and require special laundry handling. Be sure to read the label and eyeball the T before you purchase. You may need to buy a size larger than usual.

Sweatshirt – these are usually loose-fitting, made of cotton with long sleeves, and can be hooded or not. Many women enjoy having a nice sweatshirt they can throw on when they are cold or when desiring to dress casually.

Holiday – some women own special clothing they wear on certain holidays. This might include a silk blouse, a specially decorated sweatshirt or T-shirt, or something velvet. If you know your person very well, purchasing something as holiday or special-event wear would be a good choice. However, the challenge here is if you buy a special holiday garment as her holiday gift, she won't be able to wear it until the next holiday rolls around.

Miscellaneous Information on Tops

Fabrics – flannel, yarn, cotton, polyester, silk, velvet, spandex, lace, cashmere. Usually you can categorize an item based on its fabric. Flannel and cotton are often more casual items; yarn would most likely be a sweater; polyester, silk, velvet, and lace are dressier; and spandex is usually under-clothing, such as a tank top or leggings.

Sleeve length – spaghetti strap, sleeveless, cap, short, three-quarter, and long. Basically, you can get any sleeve length you are looking for. The range is the full length of the arm. Isn't that convenient?

Closures – to button or not to button? Okay, you might be thinking that this is a frivolous thing to add to the process, but it really isn't. Why? Some women, especially if they are larger on top, don't like to wear tops that button down the front because they can be too revealing. If a gap is created between the buttons, then the underclothing can be seen, and many women don't like this. When purchasing a blouse that has buttons, be careful with the sizing. Sometimes, it is better to buy a slightly larger size to be sure there will be no gaps between the buttons.

Collar line – turtleneck/high collar or low collar. Another issue can be the depth of the collar line. Some women are not comfortable wearing a blouse with a plunging neckline; they prefer the neckline a little higher up on their chest, maybe just a few inches below the collarbone to avoid any unwanted revealing. Consider the purpose of the purchase: if it is office-wear, it is usually better to be conservative. If the garment is intended to be worn in a party setting, less conservative is okay. Another thing to consider is if your special lady is a mom and has young children; quite often she will be bending over to help her children, pick them up, or pick up a toy. In this case, the collar line can be an important consideration.

BOTTOMS

Slacks/Trousers – usually made of polyester or wool and loose-fitting. Many women wear slacks or trousers to work if they are in an office environment.

Jeans – does this category even need explanation? Well, yes, it does actually. Many women love to wear jeans and many others do not. Jeans tend to be tight and constricting to some and therefore are not the most favored choice.

> "I wish I had invented blue jeans. They have expression, modesty, sex appeal, simplicity—all I hope for in my clothes."
> Yves Saint Laurent

If your person tends to prefer a looser-fitting item of clothing, jeans probably are not the best thing for you to purchase for her. However, some women like to have one pair of fashionable jeans in their closet because they want to be prepared for such an occasion when jeans are warranted. There are also trouser-type jeans that you can purchase if she prefers a relaxed fit in her clothing.

Casual Pants – for the woman who prefers the loose fit, casual pants are a great choice. They come in a variety of colors and are usually made of cotton or a cotton/polyester blend. A few popular brands on the market include Dockers, St. John's Bay, Chaps, Croft and Barrow, and DKNY.

Capris – perfect for warmer weather and for women who prefer not to wear shorts. Capris come in a variety of lengths, from those hitting just at the knee to barely above the ankle. The length of the capri should be in proportion to the height of your person. If she is on the shorter side, stick with a shorter capri. Tall women can usually get away with a longer capri. They also come in a variety of colors, fabrics, and styles, and remain a good choice for many women as a comfortable clothing item for spring and summer.

Leggings – leggings are thinner in fabric, made from a knit fabric, nylon, or spandex. They are sometimes worn under a tunic. Leggings can be an easy purchase because of the limited size and color options.

They are packaged with a height/weight range along with the accompanying size, usually small, medium, and large, and they are most times found in darker, neutral colors, such as gray, brown, navy, and black.

Loungewear/house pants/sweatpants – loungewear or house pants (sometimes referred to as pajamas) come in a variety of colors, fabrics, and prints or solids. They are a popular item, especially with the younger generation, and are usually a fairly easy purchase. They come in lettered sizes (S, M, L). Sweatpants are thicker fabric but also come in lettered sizes. Sweatpants, as sweatshirts, are a great item to have in your closet. Many women enjoy wearing them around the house, especially in the winter, to be warm and comfortable.

<u>Shorts</u> – obviously, shorts are just a shorter version of pants. They come in a variety of colors and fabrics. They can be casual or dressy. They also come in a variety of lengths, from short (just below the booty) to Bermuda (just above the knee).

<u>Skirts</u> – many women enjoy wearing skirts, especially in the spring and summer, because they are comfortable and breezy. They are also very versatile; they can be casual during the day and spruced up to be dressier in the evening. They come in a variety of fabrics, styles, and colors.

You can also purchase the length most desired or the one that looks the best on your sweetheart. Skirts are similar to capris for length preference. If she is on the petite side, a shorter skirt would most likely be the better choice. A taller woman can wear a longer skirt and it will look good.

Miscellaneous Information on Bottoms

<u>Fabrics</u> – cotton, polyester, silk, velvet/holiday, denim, and leather. Just as with tops, you can generally categorize an item based on its fabric. Cotton and denim are often more casual items; polyester, silk, and velvet would be dressier.

<u>Rise</u> – the rise is determined by the distance between the crotch seam up the zipper to the waistband. The lower the measurement, the lower the pants sit on the body. Low-rise pants have a rise between 5 and 7 inches; mid-rise is between 7 and 10 inches and high-rise is between 10 and 12 inches. Low-rise pants have been popular for many years. Most women have a preference on this aspect of their

clothing. Check her closet to see what she has purchased in the past or ask her what she prefers.

DRESSES/SUITS

Many women love to wear dresses, especially in warm weather. They are cool and comfortable and can be dressy or casual, depending on the need. Some dress options include:

Career – what she would wear in her professional life; this would usually be silk, polyester, or a wool/wool blend.

Casual – a dress most likely worn on weekends; fabrics include cotton and polyester.

Sundress – sundresses are generally casual, made of cotton or a polyester blend, and usually have thin straps rather than a full sleeve.

Special Occasion – something she might wear to a wedding, a funeral, or a special night out. Fabrics for special occasion dresses could include silk, velvet, or polyester blend. Special occasion dresses are typically not purchased often due to the nature of their need. However, if you happen to spot a beautiful dress that is the size of your special lady, go ahead and give it a try. Often a woman will turn down an opportunity to attend a special event or forego a night on the town simply because she doesn't think she has appropriate attire. You purchasing a special occasion dress for her can negate her concern.

Trendy – Trends tend to pop up quite often, which is beneficial to you. For example, a few years back, full-length casual dresses appeared on the scene. For many years, women didn't wear full-length dresses except to proms or possibly to a wedding. However, when they entered the fashion scene again, many women enjoyed their look and their popularity. You noticing trends such as this and buying her something that fits into the latest trend will wow her! Base your purchase on the information you already know about her (size, color preferences, etc.) and you'll do fine in the trendy category.

Little-black/cocktail – A little black dress is an evening or cocktail dress, cut simply and short. The little black dress is attributed originally to the 1920s designs of Coco Chanel. This wardrobe item is meant to be long-lasting, versatile, and affordable.

> "One is never over-dressed or underdressed in a little black dress."
> Karl Lagerfeld

The little black dress is considered an essential component of any woman's closet. The old rule of fashion was that every woman should own a simple, elegant black dress that could be dressed up or down depending on the occasion.

My biggest suggestion when purchasing any gift, but especially clothing, is that you *know* your person very well and buy her something that she will like and want to wear. It is important that you like it too if you want her to wear it when she is with you, but the bigger piece of the puzzle is to be as confident as possible that she will like it.

Don't buy something low-cut or low-rise if she does not wear those things and does not like them. She will not feel comfortable in the item, and you will have wasted your valuable shopping time and your money. If she likes fitted clothing, don't buy something that is loose-fitting. If she likes trouser-type pants, don't buy her skinny jeans. Follow me?

An encouraging word: if you don't get it right this time around, don't worry. I promise there will be another opportunity just around the corner to try again. You will have other chances to buy the perfect gift. You just need to practice and continue getting to know your person for who she is and what she likes.

OUTERWEAR

Basically, there are two types of outerwear: coat or jacket. Each has a specific purpose. There are a few other outerwear items that are currently in style. These include wrap, cape, and vest.

Coats

Pea Coat – The term *pea coat* originated with the Dutch and referred to a type of cloth used in making a coat worn primarily by American and European sailors. Originally, they were made of wool and were generally navy in color. However, they are now available in a range of colors and styles but still have the same basic characteristics as the original version. These outer garments are characterized mostly by broad lapels and are often double-breasted and typically fall just below the booty.

Raincoat – This category seems pretty obvious. I'm sure you know what a raincoat is and the purpose it serves. However, I want to add that rainwear can either be characterized as a coat or a jacket depending on the length. They are, of course, waterproof and are worn simply to protect the body from the elements.

Modern raincoats are often constructed of breathable, waterproof fabrics such as Gore-Tex and/or coated nylons.

Trench Coat – Some outer clothing items originated from styles the military used in its uniforms. The trench coat was originally part of an officer's uniform. For this reason, the trench coat carried a businesslike respectability and became popular for non-military people.

A typical trench coat is a ten-button, double-breasted, long coat made with tan, khaki, beige, or black fabric. It often has cuff straps on the sleeves, shoulder straps, and a belt. The trench coat was typically worn as a windbreaker or as a rain jacket, and not necessarily for protection from the cold or snow. However, many trench coats today are made with wool lining so they can be worn both as a protection from the rain and to keep the person warm.

Parka – A parka is a type of heavy coat with a hood, often lined with fleece, fur, or faux fur. Both the hood and the coat itself are lined to protect the body, head, and face from a combination of low temperatures and wind. Parkas can be categorized as arctic, mountain, and swim.

I doubt if you'll need to purchase an arctic parka (some are made to protect up to -60 F temperatures), but mountain and swim parkas could come in handy, depending on your sweetheart. Mountain parkas are intended to be worn while hiking in extreme conditions. They are protective against low temperatures, rain, and wind. They vary in length from hip to knee.

Swim parkas are usually fleece-lined, long, and hooded. Swimmers appreciate these when they exit the pool after extended sessions of training and competition.

Fabrics for coats include fur, wool, fleece, leather, faux leather, faux suede, and water-resistant materials. They can be long or short, hooded or not, but typically a *coat* denotes an item longer in length to protect more of her body.

JACKETS

Obviously, jackets fall into the outwear category. Jackets tend to be more casual than coats. There are many styles of jackets, such as denim or windbreaker. The biggest difference between a coat and a jacket is the length. Jackets usually run much shorter than coats, and most women like to have one of each option in their closet for different needs.

The general purpose of outerwear is obviously to keep the lady warm and/or protected in inclement weather. The specific purpose will depend on what the outer garment is.

Both coats and jackets can be practical or girly. Practical is a necessary item with conservative characteristics: neutral color and classic style. Girly usually serves no purpose other than to be cute: it goes with an outfit and she enjoys wearing it because it makes her look and/or feel attractive.

WRAP/CAPE/PONCHO/CLOAK

This style of cover-up was popular in the past and is now chic once again. As you can see by the heading, there are four words that can basically mean the same thing. This type of outer garment is usually light and just one piece of fabric that covers the back half of the body (but can wrap around to keep the front half warm) and fastens in some way at the neck.

The biggest difference among the terms in this category is fabric and length. A cloak is usually long, often falling below the knee, and a poncho typically denotes a type of garment worn by Native Americans or other tribal people, and is thick with a distinct fabric pattern.

Wraps/capes are often worn as evening wear by women as a fashion statement and to protect them from the elements without damaging the fine fabrics of their evening attire. Fabrics for this type of garment include velvet, silk, and satin.

At first glance, it might seem that this is a category you can ignore. You may be thinking, "Hey, we don't sit around a campfire wearing a blanket for warmth very often so I don't really need to worry about a poncho or a wrap." However, many women do enjoy going out in the evening wearing a fancy blouse and would like to have a light outer garment to wear on just such an occasion to keep their shoulders and arms protected. This is a perfect occasion for a wrap or cape.

This category could also be considered an extra or non-essential item, so purchasing a wrap would get you extra credit if you do a good job of it.

VESTS

Many women like to have a vest in their closet to use on the occasion that they feel a little chilled but don't want to wear a full jacket or coat. Vests are currently quite popular and can be found in many stores in a variety of colors, fabrics, and styles.

SCARVES

Scarves are popular these days, and lots of women wear them even when not wearing a coat. Sometimes they are worn to add a splash of color to an otherwise neutral outfit. Sometimes they are worn for warmth.

When picking out a scarf, there is really no right or wrong thing to do. Just shop to your heart's content. Buying a scarf that she will love is a pretty easy thing to do; you really can't go wrong with a scarf.

One word of caution: check her scarf inventory before shopping. Buying a scarf for a woman could be similar to buying a tie for a man. She may have too many scarves already and buying her another one may give her the idea that you didn't know what else to get so you opted for the easy way out. And we don't want her thinking that.

If she likes scarves, wears them, and has a limited supply, then go for it. But if she already has twelve scarves, she probably doesn't really want another one unless she has specifically asked for a certain type/color/style. In that case, get her a scarf that fits her needs and she'll be impressed that you listened to her scarf cues.

GLOVES/MITTENS

Scarves and gloves are sometimes sold together in a set. Those make great gifts if she needs a scarf and/or gloves. You can also buy them separately and will most likely have more selection if you take that path.

HATS

Hats are another fun item to purchase, but not all women wear them. Notice if she has ever worn a hat before you purchase one for her. If you do decide to buy a hat for her, choose the one you think she'll enjoy the most.

Similar to scarves, there is really no right or wrong choice in this category. There are lots of hats to choose from with varying types of fabric and style, and most are pretty cute, colorful, and trendy. Hats tend to cause the wearer to feel elegant or fun and hip. These are good things.

OUTERWEAR JEWELRY/ADORNMENTS

You might not have even realized there was such a thing as outerwear jewelry. This would most likely fall into the frivolous items category. They are totally girly and totally fun.

Outerwear jewelry might include a pin/broach for a coat or scarf or fuzzy cuffs for gloves. There are even fuzzy cuffs for boots that make any pair of boots fancy or different. Check out the shoe department in your local department store for boot cuffs. This is usually only a winter item, however, so they might not always be available.

SHOES

Nearly every woman loves shoes and enjoys having quite a collection in her closet. Sometimes, they might be a difficult purchase based on her feet. If she is hard to fit, shoes might not be your best choice for a gift. However, if you are confident in what she likes and you know her size, go ahead and give this category a try. Even if the shoes don't fit, you'll get credit for trying. Below is a list of the different types of footwear you might consider:

> "I did not have three thousand pairs of shoes. I had one thousand and sixty."
> Imelda Marcos

Boots – casual, dressy, high-heeled, low-heeled, ankle, pull-on, lace-up, zippered, leather, suede, faux-leather, faux-suede.

Casual Shoes – what she might wear with jeans or casual pants. Some options in this category include clogs, mules, loafers, oxfords.

Pumps – these usually have a high heel and are close-toed and close-heeled, but do not have to be. Some have a small opening for the toe while others have just a strap at the heel. Pumps are typically worn to the office, church, or an evening out on the town because they are dressier in nature.

Fancy – holiday or special-occasion shoes.

Useless or Girly – something that she'll only wear with one specific outfit or only in certain situations.

Flip-Flops – ahh, the nearly perfect shoe. Every girl needs a pair of flip-flops to just goof off in. Flip-flops tend to be a fun purchase because she knows she'll be having fun when she's wearing them, either on the beach or strolling through town, window shopping. They come in a variety of colors and patterns and are usually affordable, often under twenty dollars.

Sandals – another staple in a woman's closet is a good pair of sandals. These differ from flip-flops in that they are more supportive and will last many times longer. Sandals are great for long days of walking because they support the foot much better than the flip-flop.

> **"Give a girl the right shoes, and she can conquer the world."**
> **Marilyn Monroe**

ATHLETIC WEAR/SPORTS GEAR

If your dreamboat is active and enjoys participating in sports, there is a good chance she needs apparel appropriate for the sport or tools necessary to help her be successful. This gives you great latitude to be her hero.

There's a lot of opportunity for you to buy fabulous gifts based on her physical activities. Below is a list of possible sports she may be involved in. Though some of them may overlap with the same clothing/tools, there are some that have their own specific needs.

Ball Sports

- Tennis

- Racquetball

- Basketball

- Baseball/Softball

- Volleyball/Badminton

- Soccer

- Golf

- Ping Pong/Table Tennis

- Bocce Ball

Water Sports

- Swimming
- Water Skiing
- Scuba Diving
- Fishing
- Wind Surfing
- Water Polo
- Wakeboarding

Mountain Sports

- Hiking
- Snow Skiing
- Bobsledding
- Hang Gliding
- Trail Running

Gym Sports

- Weight Lifting/Body Building
- Classes: Spin, Aerobics, Yoga, Pilates
- Mixed Martial Arts (MMA)

Triathalon

- Running/Track and Field

- Bicycling

- Swimming

Other Sports

- Power Walking

- Dance

- Archery

- Squash

- Curling – does anyone even know what sport this is?

- Pool

- Ice Skating/Roller Blading

- Equestrian

- Skateboarding

- Gymnastics

- Fencing

- Lacrosse

- Cheerleading

- Skydiving

Don't think that you only need proper clothing for these sports. Remember, she may need special socks or shoes for the activity. What about protective gear, such as knee pads or a helmet? How about eye protection?

Another item necessary for most sports is a bag in which to carry all the paraphernalia. There are some great gear bags on the market that are specific to the sport. As you know, the right tools/gear makes any activity better. She'll love receiving something special to help her be successful in her sport of choice.

Let me give just one more helpful hint in this category. After some of these sports, she'll need to change clothes before moving into her next activity. Here is another gift-giving opportunity. Even purchasing her a nice set of lounge wear can be a great gift. If she is a swimmer, for example, she won't want to travel to her next destination in her wet swimming suit. Give her a warm, cozy sweatshirt and sweatpants to

> **"It's very important to have the right clothing to exercise in. If you throw on an old T-shirt or sweats, it's not inspiring for your workout."**
> **Cheryl Tiegs**

change into after doing her exercise laps in the pool. She'll be comfortable, and this attire will also give her muscles a chance to settle down after their workout. And again, you'll be sitting pretty because you gave her something thoughtful and useful.

INTIMATE APPAREL

Yeah, baby! Woo hoo … now we're getting to the good stuff. Intimate apparel is a fun thing to buy your special someone. But you must know what you are doing, particularly in this category. Most men think if they go to Victoria's Secret for a purchase and give their special gal one of the pink boxes or pink gift bags, they'll be a shoo-in for an Oscar in the gift-giving category. This is absolutely not true. You cannot just go in blind to a specialty store like this and rely solely on the sales clerk. She does not know your person like you do.

Use your knowledge and your desire to show her you care. Go in with some idea of what you want to purchase. You can certainly get help from the sales associate, but don't leave it all up to fate. Go in prepared. You'll be glad you did.

Does she like matching undergarments, bra and panty alike? Does she prefer comfort or will she want the newest style? Does she prefer to sleep in a gown or pajamas? Does she enjoy wearing slippers around the house?

If you live in a cold climate, does she enjoy wearing a thick fuzzy robe and slippers? Do you have an upcoming vacation to a warm locale? How about picking up a cute set of pjs she can wear around the hotel room or condo?

Keep in mind what you are aiming for with this purchase. Are you purchasing a gift for her—something she will want/like/wear—or are you really buying a gift for yourself that she'll be the wearer of? The answer to this question will dictate your purchase. Give it some thought before you go to the specialty boutique or the lingerie department in a department store.

Here are some options in this category:

- Bra

- Underwear: both sexy and practical

- Negligee: sexy nighttime apparel

- Pajamas

- Gown

- Housecoat/Robe

- Slippers

- House Socks (these usually have some sort of rubbery-type sole so they can be worn around the house and have a bit of traction)

> **"When she returned from shopping, she found this note: 'Sweetheart, you'll find my Valentine gift to you on the bed.' She ran upstairs. On the bed, fast asleep, was her husband."**

SIZING

Some of this information may seem silly to share. However, I want to make this process as easy as possible for you, so I've included some things you may already know, like explaining T-shirts and sweatpants.

When it comes to clothing, there are several sizing options. These include: junior, misses, petite, tall, plus size, and maternity. These categories cover nearly all clothing items: tops, bottoms, intimate apparel, and outerwear. This would not include shoes or miscellaneous items, such as hats, scarves, and gloves.

Typical sizing can either be letters—S, M, L—or numbers—2, 4, 6. Shopping by letter is fairly easy and straightforward. Your choices are small (S), medium (M), large (L), and extra-large (XL). The number system is a tad trickier but still learnable.

When shopping in a junior section of a department store or in a junior-based store (Pac Sun, Forever 21, Charlotte Russe, Tilly's, etc.) the numbered sizing is in odd numbers. This is how you know it is a junior size. The odd numbers 1 through 17 will be found in a junior store or a junior department. The smaller the number, the smaller the size. Junior clothing is also cut somewhat smaller than misses clothing. Since juniors tend to have smaller body frames and also have differing fashion taste, that clothing tends to have a straighter cut for a tighter fit. The sizing does not necessarily coordinate between juniors and misses. For example, a size 0 in juniors will be slightly smaller than a size 0 in misses.

When shopping in the woman's section, there are usually four choices: petites (5'4" and under), misses, tall (5'8" and over), and plus size (or full-figure). The petite, misses, and tall sections include the even numbers of 0 through 16. The plus size or full-figure department will have even numbers above 16. Juniors, misses, petite, and tall have the number zero and it denotes a very small size, a number I haven't seen since I was twelve.

There is one other sizing option, and that is called no-size or one-size. This means that the manufacturer assumes everyone is the same size. Of course we know this is not true. Sometimes, tank tops are sized in this manner. Be careful when purchasing items with the no-size or one-size labeling. It may not work for your person.

A quick word of advice: when in doubt, do *not* be generous with sizing (except in the situations listed previously). By this I mean, if you think she is a size 8 but aren't positive, it is not necessarily better to go up in size, say to a size 10. If you think she is a small but you buy a medium, this is not always a good choice.

Women do not want you to think they are bigger than they are. It will nearly always be a better choice to go smaller rather than larger. When in doubt, go low.

The sizing on bottoms is similar to the sizing on tops. However, unless it is a pair of leggings or lounge pants, you probably will not see the letter system used. Bottoms are nearly always sold using the numbering system.

Jeans sometimes are sized according to waist measurements rather than the numbered system explained above. So rather than using the 2, 4, 6 numbering system, jeans can be sized 26, 28, 30, etc. Below is a simple conversion chart that should be helpful:

WOMEN'S SIZING:

U.S. and Canada	Europe	U.K.	Australia	Japan
2	32	4	6	5
4	34	6	8	7
6	36	8	10	9
8	38	10	12	11
10	40	12	14	13
12	42	14	16	15
14	44	16	18	17

JUNIOR SIZING:

U.S. and Canada	Europe	U.K. and Australia	Japan
1	28	3	0
3	30	5	2
5	32	7	4
7	34	9	6
9	36	11	8
11	38	13	10
13	40	15	12
15	42	17	14

PLUS SIZING:

U.S. and Canada	Europe	U.K.	Australia	Japan
16	46	18	20	19
18	48	20	22	21
20	50	22	24	23
22	52	24	26	25
24	54	26	28	27
26	56	28	30	29
28	58	30	32	31

Dresses can come in the lettering system but most often will be sized according to the number system mentioned previously. Most women will wear the same size dress as they do other clothing items. For example, if she wears a size 8 blouse or pant, she'll wear a size 8 dress. The same goes for a suit.

Keep in mind however, that a suit, since it is usually bought together, both top and bottom, can be difficult to purchase for your person. If she is not the same size on both top and bottom, it might be best to stick with buying separates for her.

Generally speaking, women's shoes come in sizes 5–10, both full and half sizes. For example: 5, 5 1/2, 6, 6 1/2, etc. Some specialty shoe stores as well as large department stores, such as Nordstrom and Macy's, carry smaller sizes like 4 and 4 1/2 and sizes above 10. Most women's shoes come in three basic widths: narrow, medium, and wide. Again, some brands may carry a slim or 2A/3A (very narrow), but many do not.

SHOE SIZING:

U.S.	5	5½	6	6½	7	7½	8	8½
European	36	36½	37	37½	38	38½	39	39½

U.S.	9	9½	10	10½	11	11½	12
European	40	40½	41	41½	42	42½	43

AAHHH! JEWELRY

Nearly every woman loves jewelry. Even if a woman doesn't wear much jewelry, she does wear some, at the very least a watch. This gives you great latitude when looking to purchase jewelry. Some women prefer to wear only fine jewelry, but with the quality of today's fashion jewelry, you have much greater variety than in years gone by. Go into any department store and you'll find a myriad of turntables offering a vast array of jewelry options, including:

- Rings

- Earrings

- Necklaces

- Bracelets

- Charms (both necklaces and bracelets)

- Anklets

- Toe Rings

- Body Jewelry: ear cuffs, belly button rings

- Watches

- Toe Thongs (for tropical locations)

When purchasing a ring, you will need to know her size. For example, fashion rings range from size 5 to size 10 (in whole sizes only). Fine jewelry, jewelry purchased from a dedicated jewelry store or a jewelry department in large department stores, most often come in a 7 or 7 1/2 but can be adjusted when necessary.

With regard to earrings, there are basically two things to consider. One concern is the weight. Some women don't like wearing heavy earrings because they pull on their earlobe. Test the weight of the earring in the store before you purchase.

The second consideration is the form of the earring. Does she have pierced ears or does she wear clip-ons? If your petunia does not have pierced ears, then you'll need to look for clip-on style earrings.

Necklace lengths and terms are as follows:

- 13" to 16" is called the *collar and choker* lengths and should be comfortably close-fitting, lying above the collar bone.

- 17" to 19" is the *princess* length and is the most common length, which rests just over the collar bone.

- 20" to 24" is the *matinee* and is usually a drape of beads on the chest.

- 28" to 32" is called *opera* length. It drapes to the mid-section.

- Over 45" is the *lariat* or *rope*, a long string of beads that can be looped, wrapped, or draped.

Charms can either be for a necklace or a bracelet. One specialty charm bracelet is called Pandora. You can do an online search under the name Pandora to buy online or find a local brick-and-mortar store to purchase it from. There are several other types of charm bracelets as well. Many jewelry stores are now offering their own charm bracelets/necklaces. For example, Kay's Jewelers has one called *Charmed Memories*, and Zales has named their charms *Persona*. Tiffany and Co.'s version is called *Charmed by Tiffany*.

The great thing about buying a charm-type gift is that it gives you ample gift ideas for the future. For example, you decide you want to start a charm bracelet for her. For this first purchase, you can buy the actual bracelet and one or two charms and leave it at that. The next gift-buying opportunity you have, buy her another charm. Not only will you be able to fill her bracelet, others can do so as well. It enables her to have a gift now, plus something to look forward to.

Anklets or ankle bracelets also come in a variety of lengths from seven to twelve inches. Sizing on anklets is important. If it is too short, it will break when she flexes her foot. If it is too long, it will fall below her ankle bone and hinder her ability to walk. You may need to measure her ankle to get the accurate size.

> **"Jewelry takes people's minds off your wrinkles."**
> **Sonja Henie**

BATH/BODY

I imagine you will know what falls into this category: the stuff that smells yummy, the stuff that makes her skin soft, the stuff that makes her feel pampered.

<u>Body Moisturizers</u> – this would include lotion, cream, and body butter. Lotions have a low-to medium-viscosity and are intended for topical application to unbroken skin. Many lotions, especially for the hands and face, are formulated to smooth, rehydrate, and soften the skin. Some lotions may contain fragrances. By contrast, creams and butters are much thicker, but their intended use is still the same—hydration and softening of the skin.

<u>Fragrances</u> – this would include eau de cologne, eau de toilette, eau de parfum, and perfume. A new category is now available called body spritz. Let's have a quick lesson in the difference in fragrance types.

Eau de cologne is at the bottom end of the range as far as concentration is concerned and usually contains about seven percent oil essence. You can usually get this type in a large size. It is often applied by spray. This type also tends to be the most cost effective of the options.

Eau de toilette can contain up to ten percent aromatic essence. Eau de toilette is the most popular form in which a fragrance is sold.

Eau de parfum is the next in line. The concentration of oils is over fifteen percent, sometimes reaching as high as twenty percent. Since it is less intense than perfume extract, it is also cheaper and is sold in small sizes.

Perfume is the most expensive version of any fragrance. This is due to the high concentration of essence, as much as forty percent by volume. Because of the high volume of essence oil, perfume is the longest lasting of all the scent categories.

> "Two things make the women unforgettable, their tears and their perfume."
> Sacha Guitry

Body mists and body spritzers have become popular in recent years due to their light scent and reasonable cost. A mist is usually scent-free but has some essential oil in it. She would use it after a shower to rehydrate her skin. A spritz does have scent and would be used similar to a perfume. Spritzes tend to have very little oil essence and can be spritzed on when a perfume would be too overpowering. Many women use a spritzer when going to the gym or a yoga class or when they'll be around a large group of people in an enclosed space, such as an airplane or subway.

Bath Salts – the term bath salts refers to a range of water-soluble products designed to be added to a bath, although that explanation is probably obvious. They are said to improve cleaning, enhance the experience of bathing, serve as a vehicle for cosmetic agents, and some even claim medicinal benefits. Fragrances and colors are often added to bath salts.

Shower Gel – shower gels are basically a liquid soap available in a variety of scents. Some shower gels are herb-infused, and some offer aromatherapeutic benefits. Shower gels work best with the bath mesh, which removes dead skin cells, sweat, and dirt.

<u>Body Scrub</u> – this great product exfoliates the dead skin cells and aids in the generation of new ones. Body scrubs use a variety of ingredients in order to exfoliate the skin, some more harsh than others. Options include sugar granules, fruit seeds, nut shells, ground rice, and fruit peels. These are mixed with oils to create the scrub that will leave the skin feeling soft and rejuvenated. Pay close attention to your sweetie-pie's skin and sensitivity to scrubs. Some are too harsh while others can have little exfoliating effect. Just ask her which type she prefers. I'm sure she'll be glad to share her favorite brand, scent, and type so you can be sure to buy her the right stuff.

<u>Room Air Fresheners</u> – I'm not talking about buying her a can of spray air freshener, silly man. Room air fresheners come in a variety of colors, styles, and scents. They can be found at stores such as Bath and Body Works, The Body Shop, and Bed, Bath & Beyond, as well as at pharmacy-type stores, such as CVS, Walgreens, and Rite Aid.

<u>Drawer Sachets/Perfumed Drawer Liners</u> – a sachet is a small bag of perfumed herbs and flowers used in drawers and cedar chests to keep contents fragrant. A perfumed drawer liner is similar to contact paper you would use in the kitchen, only it is perfumed. The intent again is to keep the contents of the drawer fragrant.

There is a wide variety of scents available. These can be found online, under "perfumed drawer liners/scented drawer liners," or in stores such as Bed, Bath & Beyond, The Container Store, and Crabtree & Evelyn.

You can go into bath/body specialty stores and receive assistance, but as I mentioned before, don't go in without some knowledge of what she might like. Does she take baths often enough to warrant the purchase of bath salts? Does she like lotions, or is her skin sensitive so that she needs a special blend of lotion or perfume in order not to react negatively? Does she use shower gel or does she prefer a bar of soap? Does she have a favorite perfume scent?

As an added bonus, several of these specialty stores offer a frequent buyer card. Once you make your purchase, you can sign up for this benefit and give the card to her for future purchases. Some even offer free products for special occasions, such as birthdays or anniversaries. Just ask your friendly sales clerk if her store offers such an item. Having a frequent buyer card will help you in future purchases and will also save you money.

HANDBAGS

Purses or handbags sometimes are too personal of an item for someone else to purchase, and many women like to shop for one themselves because they know the special features they desire in a handbag. However, if you are out shopping and you see something that catches your eye, don't be afraid to venture into this category. There are many choices. Below are a few of the popular types of handbags that you could choose:

Backpack – I'm sure you are familiar with the backpack. You might even own one yourself. However, there is also a backpack handbag. They've been popular for quite some time because they are comfortable to carry. The backpack handbag is made with the two straps similar to a traditional backpack so that it can be carried in the same manner. However, rather than having one large opening, this backpack usually has several compartments and is smaller than the traditional backpack.

Clutch Bag – the clutch is usually worn in the evening for special occasions or when she doesn't want to carry a large handbag. They most often are long and shallow with a clasp or a fold-over closure. Many clutch bags do not have a strap but are simply carried in the hand. They tend to have a small interior and are meant to only carry the essentials, such as lipstick and a cell phone.

<u>Hobos</u> – a hobo bag is one that tends to have shorter straps and is made of soft leather or cloth so that it can create a slouchy posture.

<u>Satchel</u> – a satchel is a bag with a strap, usually worn diagonally across the body, with the bag hanging on the opposite hip, rather than hanging directly down from the shoulder. It is traditionally used for carrying books but has become popular due to its versatility and comfort.

<u>Shoulder Bag</u> – a shoulder bag is probably the most generic term and most popular type of bag. It is simply a purse with straps at a length that cause the bag to sit at or near the waist.

<u>Tote Bag</u> – usually carried as an addition to a purse. Tote bags are bigger than most purses and can carry books, snacks, water, coupons, or other miscellaneous items that a woman might need during her time away from home but most likely are things she doesn't want to carry in her purse. Totes come in very handy because of their size and durability.

<u>Wristlet</u> – this style of handbag has been around for a while but has gone by several different names. At one point, it was called a wallet on a string. A wristlet is basically a wallet with a short strap, usually attached to the side. It is meant to be carried by having the strap around her wrist with the wallet held by the hand. They are a no-fuss type of bag and are enjoyed by women who prefer to only carry the basics, such as identification and credit cards.

<u>Waist Bag/Fanny Pack</u> – a waist bag is one that has a belt-type strap and is worn around the waist. This type of bag is worn when it is important to have your hands free but you still need to have essential items available. Women would most likely choose to wear this type of bag when doing a fund-raising type walk/run, hiking, or participating in another outdoor activity.

The bonus of choosing a handbag as your gift of choice is that there are so many options: color, style, fabric, size. Many women have an array of handbags in their closet, so odds are good that even if you don't buy something she will carry every day, you will be able to pick something that she'll be able to use on occasion.

> **"Is that weird, taking my Louis Vuitton bag camping?"**
> **Jessica Simpson**

OTHER PERSONAL ITEMS

Some of the following items might appear to be too personal for you to purchase. However, as long as you know your gal (am I harping on this point too much?) you can still pick out a few goodies from this list and get a positive reaction from her. For example, brush kits and nail kits are good purchases. Below is a list of other personal item options:

- Makeup

- Nail Polish

- Hair Accessories

- Hosiery

- Beauty Application Tools (brushes, nail kits)

- Belt

- Luggage

Many beauty stores, such as The Body Shop and Bath and Body Works, put together nice gift sets. Or you could put a beauty basket together yourself from the local pharmacy store. This might include a mascara, a brush set (for applying makeup), and a bottle of neutral nail polish.

If you pay attention to what she normally uses or wears, it won't be too difficult to create a personalized gift. Does she wear hair accessories? Does she like neutral colors in her makeup, like browns and taupes for eyes and rose for cheeks? Or does she like brighter colors, like blues and greens for eye shadow and pinks for her cheeks?

There are other specialty stores, such as Brighton, Coach, and Vera Bradley, that have an array of beautiful personal and travel specialty items, such as handbags/travel bags, belts, and luggage.

READING MATERIAL

There are so many books and magazines out there to choose from as possible gifts for your honey. First, you need to know if she likes to read books and/or flip through magazines. Your second goal is to find out what types of books and magazines interest her: hobbies, sports, current events, etc. Third, decide if you want a one-time gift or something that will last a little longer.

Books – some categories to consider:

- Fiction/Novel

  ◊ Romance

  ◊ Soulful Stories

  ◊ Mystery/Thrillers

- Non-Fiction

  ◊ Biographies

  ◊ Memoirs

- History

- Health and Nutrition

- Poetry

- Food and Wine

- Cookbooks

> "A classic is something that everybody wants to have read and nobody wants to read."
> Mark Twain

- Literature

- Sports

- How-To

- Art and Photography

- Business

- Entertainment

- Home/Garden

- Nature

- Parenting

- Religion/Spirituality

- Travel

There are many on-line book sites if you prefer to shop from the comfort of your home. These include Barnes & Noble, Amazon, and half.com (a division of eBay). There are also independent bookstores that have a web presence and would greatly appreciate your business. Many of these local sellers also offer used books, which can usually be purchased at a lower price.

If you'd like to go the magazine route, you can either buy her a single magazine and put it in her stocking at Christmas or sign her up for an annual subscription so that she continues to receive the magazine long after the holiday or special occasion is over. This will remind her each month of you. Score!

<u>Magazines</u> – currently, there are over twenty-four thousand magazine titles for you to choose from. Wow! Now that's a lot of gift opportunities.

- Sports and Recreation – *Sports Illustrated, Snowboarding*

- Health and Fitness – *Shape, Fitness, Runner's World*

- Entertainment and TV – *People, US, Rolling Stone*

- Hobbies – *Crafters World, Creating Keepsakes, American Woodworker*

- Business and Finance – *The Economist, Harvard Business Review*

- Cooking and Food – *Cooking Light, Taste of Home*

- Home and Gardening – *House Beautiful, Garden Design*

- Photography/Art – *Shutterbug, Antiques & Fine Art*

- Religion – *Guideposts, Significant Living*

- Science/Nature – *Mother Earth News, Bird Talk*

- Antiques and Collectibles – *Country Sampler, Rock & Gem*

- Bridal – *Brides, Bridal Guide*

- Fashion – *People, Cosmo, Glamour, Vogue*

- Enrichment – *Time, Poets &Writers, Mental Floss*

- Animals/Pets – *Dog World, Audubon*

- Music – *Billboard, American Songwriter*

- Politics – *Campaigns & Elections, Time*

- Parenting – *Parenting, Parent & Child*

- Lifestyle – *Travel + Leisure, Adventure*

- Local/Regional – *Coastal Living, Cape Cod, Vermont Life*

As you can see, I listed only a few in each category. If this is a category you are interested in pursuing as a gift idea, go to a magazine website to get a full idea of your options. There are lots of sites to shop, and they make it simple to choose and purchase. Then they do the rest of the work. Look how easy that was.

And don't forget, in this age of technology, you can buy her a book on tape or an e-book, which is downloaded to her electronic reader (if she has one). Speaking of electronic readers, there is another gift idea—an electronic reader. There are several on the market: Amazon Kindle, Barnes & Noble's Nook, Sony Reader. This is a great gift idea, especially if she travels a lot or commutes to her job.

> **"Reading is to the mind what exercise is to the body."**
> **Sir Richard Steele**

ENTERTAINMENT – MUSIC, MOVIES, TV

Here's another fun category with which you could do a lot. In terms of entertainment, there is a vast array of options. You could buy her music in the form of a CD, or you could splurge and buy tickets to a concert. You could buy a DVD set of her favorite TV program, such as *Friends* or *SVU*. You could buy her a movie on DVD or take her to see a live play.

There's the opera, the symphony, the ballet, plays at community colleges or community theaters. Many women enjoy an evening splurge with a night out on the town. If you purchase tickets to a special entertaining event and throw in dinner to her favorite restaurant, you, my man, will have done well.

A good site to explore is www.imdb.com (Internet Movie Database). If you know a certain actor or actress she likes, this site reveals what work they've done. For example, you know she likes Drew Barrymore or Tom Hanks. Go to this database and you'll see the movies they've been in and then decide if you want to buy one of those films as a gift.

This site also lists movies according to genres, so if you know she likes animated movies or musicals, for example, imdb.com can help you narrow down your choices by listing movies in those, as well as many other, categories.

A friend tells this story: "Take a trip back in time to late 1978. My favorite band, Boston, was scheduled to play at McNichols Arena in Denver. I was a newly licensed driver and knew my folks would never let me make the drive from Boulder by myself. Deciding that the chances of my parents subjecting their auditory nerves to a rock concert were slim, and getting them to drive me there and hang around until after the show were even slimmer, I resigned myself to not going to the concert.

About a week before the concert, my mom shows up with two tickets to the concert. Said she was passing the TicketMaster booth, recognized the name of the group, thought I might be interested in going, and bought two tickets. I was allowed to drive myself there (with my high school sweetie) if I successfully passed a trial run with my dad. My first rock concert, first solo drive to the big city, and a gift I'll never forget." DB

ANIMALS/PETS

Okay, this category is slightly more difficult than the others. Since you are dealing with a living, breathing creature, you must be sure you are making a good choice. Receiving a cute and cuddly kitty or puppy is all well and good, but be sure that it is appropriate for the receiver and that she is ready for such a gift. If she hints she wants an animal as a gift, do all the research necessary in order to make the best choice possible. I have included this category because I do believe animals make wonderful gifts. However, I would strongly suggest that this be a purchase you make together to be absolutely sure you are making a good choice.

Some pet choices include:

- Dog/Puppy

- Cat/Kitten

- Bird

- Reptile and Amphibian (snake, lizard, frog, turtle)

- Rodents (guinea pig, gerbil, hamster)

- Fish

- Rabbit

- Hermit Crab

- Horse

HOBBIES

There are certainly lots of opportunities to buy a gift based on a hobby she has. There are so many hobbies, and I'm sure your significant other enjoys at least one of them. Some options include:

- Sports

- Crafts (scrapbooking, knitting, crochet, needlepoint, cross-stitch, ceramics/pottery, woodworking, jewelry making, candle-making, calligraphy, quilting, sewing)

- Equestrian

- Photography

- Shopping

- Reading

- Movies

- TV

- Music

- Glass-blowing

- Gardening

- Cooking/Baking

- Collecting (dolls, stamps, coins, etc.)

- Beadwork

- Electronic Games

- Board Games

- Puzzles

- Playing a Musical Instrument

- Genealogy

So where does this fit into gift-giving? Take stock in the hobbies your sweetie engages in or look over the list. What comes to mind? Does she need supplies or tools? Is there a local studio you could rent time from for her (photography, ceramics/pottery)? Are there additional classes she could take to learn more? Does she want a specialty cookbook or new baking sheets? Keep in mind that whenever you give a gift that is somewhat out of the ordinary, you may need to spruce it up a little. Let's use gardening as an example. Say your honey likes to garden and needs some new tools. Rather than just buying her a new shovel or rake, which probably won't send a warm and fuzzy message to her, why not put together a gardening gift pack? You could still give her the shovel but also include some cute gloves, perhaps a new plant, or even some garden stones with inspirational sayings on them. By doing this, you will be sending a completely different message. You are now showing her that you know she likes gardening and you want her hobby to be as successful as possible. You aren't just giving her a work tool. Understand? By delving into this category and possibly providing a gift associated with one of her leisure activities, you are showing support for what she enjoys doing.

MISCELLANEOUS

A comment overheard at a local CVS Pharmacy on Christmas Eve between a father and young son: "Dad, I don't know what to get Mom for Christmas."

This conversation is a great example of what I was referring to at the beginning of the book. If you take your kids shopping for their mother, you are doing them a great service. They learn early the importance of planning ahead, of giving thought to their actions, and you create a tradition between you and your child.

If, however, you find yourself in an emergency on Christmas Eve or birthday eve, in a pharmacy, below is a list of possible gift ideas. These are great items to consider. I strongly suggest, however, that you don't revert to this emergency situation too often. It could create the idea of "it's good enough" and make the receiver feel that not much thought was put into her personal happiness.

Below is a list of suggestions, but I also recommend you walk around the store before making your final purchase. You may find something not on this list that is a perfect gift. Use your imagination and do the best you can with this last-minute purchase.

- Sunglasses

- Wallet

- Key Ring

- Stationery

- Travel or Cosmetics Bag

- Umbrella

- Photo Frames (traditional or digital)

- Plaque with Cute Quotes

- Matching Pen and Pencil Set

- Basket of Goodies (chocolates, mints, gum, magazine)

SPECIALTY

- Engraved Gifts

- Cause-related Gifts – cancer t-shirt or ball cap, blanket, etc.

- Knickknacks (Lilliput Lane, Lladro, Disney, Swarovski, etc.)

- Sports Jerseys of Her Favorite Team

- Paraphernalia from Her Favorite Movie or TV Program

- Memories (an activity day)

Daisies are Delightful, even though they die

- Girly Gifts (fancy work gloves, fuzzy cuffs for gloves or boots)

- A Day at the Spa (manicure, pedicure, massage)

- Maid Service (house-cleaning for a special occasion)

- Flowers (even though the flowers die, many women still enjoy receiving them)

Let me explain the girly items in a little more detail. Some stores and websites sell beautiful items that may seem totally useless to you.

These stores have a plethora of treats that your sweetheart is most likely not willing to buy for herself.

My idea of the girly category is anything that is a total splurge, something she would likely feel guilty about buying for herself but would love to have. This is where you come in. You can buy her something that might seem to have no value whatsoever but it is a fun item. If you can get beyond the idea that everything you purchase needs to have a purpose, you'll do fine with this. Just know the purpose of this category is to make her smile—nothing more, nothing less.

There are more than a few websites that have extraordinary gift ideas that are slightly unusual. Café Press is one that offers team T-shirts, jerseys, mugs, and bags for sports teams as well as cause-related clothing (breast cancer, MS, etc.). For other specialty gift options, check into sites such as Zazzle, tenthousandvillages, vat19, redenvelope, giftinggrace, as well as hundreds of others. If you type *unique gifts* into any search engine, it will offer gobs of sites to investigate. You can also refine your search to *unique home décor, luxury gifts, unique gifts for the woman who has everything,* etc. There are so many online shopping sites that offer a host of options for a gift for the woman in your life. Spend some time perusing these sites and you'll be able to find something that is a perfect fit for your sweetie-pie.

One last suggestion in this category is xperiencedays.com. This site has daily activities—boating, wine tasting, helicopter tours, and race car driving —as well as train rides and city tours for a variety of cities around the country. Keep in mind, the gift does not need to be tangible. You can offer her an experience as a gift and you'll both be able to enjoy it.

TRADITIONAL GIFTS

- Jewelry

- Journals/Family Tree Information

- Start Your Own Tradition?

Traditional gifts have so much meaning. You may already have a tradition in your family, or you might like to start a tradition of your own.

Here are a few examples:

> Dan was searching for a unique gift for his oldest granddaughter, Sierra—a gift that would have special meaning to both of them. He lives in Oklahoma and Sierra lives in Utah. Upon considering the gift choices, Dan decided upon a cookbook. But it wasn't just any cookbook. It was written by Trisha Yearwood, *A Georgia Cook in an Oklahoma Kitchen*. The book had special meaning for several reasons. Trisha is married to Garth Brooks, and they are both successful country performers who live in Oklahoma, close to where Dan lives. Dan enjoys country music and loves anything to do with Oklahoma. He was proud to get such a gift for his oldest granddaughter so that he could share with her a little bit of himself in the gift.

✳ ✳ ✳

Julie R's family passes down jewelry from one generation to the next. Julie's grandmother gave her daughter, Julie's mother, a piece of jewelry, which in turn was passed down to Julie at the age of twenty-one. Julie now has a daughter, Lily, who will receive the same piece of jewelry when she turns twenty-one. Once Lily receives it, it will have passed through four generations. I'd say that's pretty special and a heart-warming gifting tradition.

Another friend, Julie M., tells me she is creating a scrapbook for each of her three daughters. Not only is she creating the photo albums with pictures of them growing up, each year she writes a letter to each daughter describing her important milestones or memories created that had special meaning to Julie. What an awesome gift those girls will get in the future.

GIFT CARDS

Gift cards are a great gift but on the surface might seem impersonal. However, if you put just a little thought into this category, you can provide a personalized gift. Does she have a favorite eatery or coffee spot? What about a favored specialty store?

There are lots of neighborhood shops and eateries that would appreciate your future business and gladly sell gift cards for future use. Consider yogurt shops and jewelry stores as well. The gift card category is one that allows you much leeway in creativity.

"I put together a gift basket for my sweetie, who was taking a Spanish class. I found a set of flash cards with Spanish terms and sayings. I also found a nice bottle of Napa Valley wine with a Spanish theme/Spanish label. Next I added a gift card to a favorite Mexican restaurant and *voila*, I had a personalized and creative gift." VJ

HOMEMADE GIFTS

If you have a creative hobby, like woodworking, obviously you could create a nice handmade gift. Other options include coupons for date night, work to be done around the house that she might normally do (washing the car or the dishes, doing the laundry, dusting, vacuuming), or watching the kids while she has a free day.

> "I love giving homemade gifts. Which one of my children would you like?"

TABOO GIFTS

Bathing Suits

A bathing suit is one of the few items I would suggest you *not* purchase. It is usually best left for the individual person to buy for herself. It is too difficult to pick something out that will fit and she will like. Usually, bathing suits are non-returnable, and you don't want to waste money on something that may not be a good purchase.

However, related things are okay, such as a swimsuit cover-up, flip-flops, a beach bag, or a beach towel.

Practical Items

- Vacuum Cleaner

- Anything for the Kitchen

- Something for Her Car

- Fixing something Broken in the House/Car

- Home Remodeling Projects

- Yard Work

- Being Nice for the Day

Okay, I'm just going to say it … these are not favored gifts for holidays, birthdays, or special occasions. If she needs a new vacuum cleaner, buy one but don't make it her birthday present. If something is broken, fix it but don't tell her it is part of her Christmas present.

Generally speaking, practical things are not something your average woman wants as a gift. She might need them, she will probably even benefit from having them, but they are not really considered gifts in her mind. Unless it is a special situation and you have previously discussed it, don't buy a vacuum cleaner, an iron, or a washing machine and call it her special gift. It's just not a good idea.

In the movie *Overboard*, Goldie Hawn receives a washing machine for her birthday. She is thrilled because she'd been using the old-fashioned type of washer and she knew this new machine would save her loads of energy and effort (pun intended) when doing the laundry for a family of six. Unless you are in a similar situation, don't buy the practical gift. They are just no fun at all.

<u>Gym Membership</u>

Don't freak out yet ... let me explain. Earlier we discussed sports and purchasing items for her that will aid in her sport of choice, such as shoes or equipment. This is totally different from buying her a gym membership or a piece of home gym equipment. Unless you discussed it previously and/or she specifically told you she wants to join a gym or desires a treadmill she can use at home, this is a taboo gift. It just sends the wrong message. Are you giving her a gym membership because you think she needs to exercise? Not a good message. Stay clear and all will be right with the world.

INTRINSICALLY VALUED GIFTS

You knew it had to happen at some point during the book, and here it is. I've waited till the end to share this idea with you. I've had such a good time writing this book and sharing with you ideas and suggestions for purchasing gifts for your honey. Now I have one last idea, and for some of you it could be the best.

Many women have all they want or need. Their kitchen is stocked with all the gadgets and their house is beautifully decorated. They have enough clothes in their closet to dress themselves for a month without duplicating items. The jewelry box is full, and the running shoes are still new. What they really want now is to reach out to someone else, someone who might not have all the things they need. Here is where you come in with a gift that does not involve a trip to the mall or any sort of internet shopping.

Intrinsically valued gifts are those that will make her feel good inside, something that will allow her to reach out beyond herself and help someone else. Some options include:

- Donate to her favorite charity in her name

- Participate in a bowl-a-thon to raise money for foster children

- Walk 39 miles in the Avon Walk for Breast Cancer

- Participate in the Relay for Life, American Cancer Society

- Donate time to your local animal shelter

- Volunteer time to a children's reading hour at your local library

- Spend some time in a senior retirement community

- Run a 5k to benefit the Leukemia and Lymphoma Society

Obviously, this list could be endless, so find out what is near and dear to her heart and contribute time and/or money to that cause. She will love you for the effort, and you'll both feel good about giving back to your community in a tangible way, especially if you contribute together. And, as an added bonus, no shopping was involved.

One final type of intrinsically valued gift is no gift at all. Is your special lady a stay-at-home mom? Would she prefer you put money into your savings account or pay off a bill rather than spend that money on a gift? I'm by no means suggesting you ignore a special day in her life by not purchasing a gift. What I am saying is that if she is worried about money and would prefer to forego a gift at a specific time for a greater long-term good, that is totally fine. Listen to her cues and pay attention to what is happening around her. If this is an avenue that will benefit her (and you/your family), then buy her a nice card to celebrate her special occasion and then discuss your decision with her. In many situations, this would be not only acceptable, but also appreciated.

> **"The most beautiful clothes that can dress a woman are the arms of the man she loves."**
> **Yves Saint-Laurent**

Final Thoughts

My fervent desire is, first, that you buy this book (I need to go shopping), and second, that you use it as a catalyst for many successful years of gift-giving. As I hope you learned through reading this little book, you'll see there are many opportunities for you to make a purchase for your significant other that will make her feel special and loved by you. I also hope you enjoyed learning how to make shopping an activity that, while you may never look forward to, you will at least be able to do with the pleasure of knowing you will be showing your sweetie-pie that you love her.

Happy shopping, my friend. Wishing you many successful gift-giving moments ahead.

For Ladies Only

Hi, ladies.

I want to spend a few minutes with you. This book is about giving your guy information, ideas, and suggestions for gifts for you. I hope I succeeded in my efforts to help him be better informed when it comes to giving you a gift. There are a few points you should consider as well, things that I believe will be helpful to the special man in your life.

Let's assume your man *wants* to do a good job at shopping and buying you a gift. Might I suggest that you give him some helpful tools to accomplish that goal?

At the end of this book is a cheat sheet. Please make a copy of these pages and fill them out. Give them to your guy and discuss the items on the list. Give him any details you'd like him to know. Help him be successful. In the end, whatever additional information you can give him will benefit you.

Keep in mind that great gifts do not necessarily equate to expensive or extravagant gifts. Great gifts are ones that show you, the recipient, that effort was put forth to provide you with something special. Please consider your guy's feelings and the effort he expended when you open the gift from him.

I'm sure there will be times when you don't like or need what he has purchased for you. However, I wrote this book to encourage men to shop for their women with a greater sense of purpose. I suggested they explore getting to know you better in the process so that they'll better understand what you might want, the things you like. Any encouragement you can give your man in this area will be good. Fill out the cheat sheet; give him lists and hints as to what you want. Then be happy and acknowledge his efforts. Your encouragement will go a long way.

Two additional things to consider:

First, you buying something you want or need and calling it a gift from him; and second, you buying what you want or need throughout the year and not really expecting anything at the holiday or on your birthday/anniversary.

While both of these issues may seem harmless, I don't think they are. I'm not suggesting that you can never buy anything for yourself again. I'm just saying that if you do intend to buy your own gift, at the very least have your special someone with you and get his input.

If you want a new dress, for example, and your birthday is coming up, tell him you want a new dress and you'd like him to shop with you at your favorite boutique to get his input on the decision (and pay the bill). This will accomplish two things: you will actually feel like you got a gift, and he'll be happy that you included him in the process. Both are great for building a healthy relationship.

Regarding the second point, I am certainly not a believer of consumerism just for the sake of consumerism. If you supply most of your wants/needs during the year, that is fine. However, as it is getting close to a gift-giving opportunity, leave something unpurchased so that he can get it for you. Leave it on your list. Make it easy for him to be able to supply you with that item. It will make him feel so much better in the long run if he is able to buy you a gift without your direct knowledge.

And have fun with him during this process. I imagine you enjoy giving special gifts to your friends and loved ones. Consider how you feel when you find that perfect gift. Help your guy create that same feeling for himself. At the end of the day, you'll be glad you did.

Sincerely,

Brenda

Cheat Sheet

DATE:

CLOTHING

TOPS:
- Blouse
- Shirt
- Tank
- Tunic
- Sweater
- T-Shirt
- Sweatshirt
- Holiday

Preferences: Size, Fabrics, Sleeve Length, Closures, and Collar Line. Do you have a favorite brand or favorite store? Do you need something specific? Give as much detail as you can.

Special Notes:

BOTTOMS:
- Slacks/Trousers
- Jeans
- Casual Pants
- Capris
- Leggings
- Loungewear/Sweatpants
- Shorts
- Skirts

Preferences: Size, Fabrics and Rise, Skinny or Relaxed? Give as much detail as you can.

Special Notes:

DRESSES:
- Career
- Casual
- Sundress
- Special Occasion
- Trendy
- Little Black/Cocktail

SUITS
Special Notes: Include size

OUTERWEAR:

- Coat – what type of coat– preferred fabric, color, style, length
- Jacket
- Wrap
- Vest
- Scarves
- Gloves
- Mittens
- Hats
- Outerwear Jewelry

Do you need something specific in this category, such as a pair of black gloves or a red scarf? Give detailed information!

Special Notes: Include size

SHOES:

- Boots
- Casual Shoes
- Pumps
- Fancy
- Girly
- Flip-Flops
- Sandals

Special Notes: Include size

ATHLETIC WEAR/SPORTS GEAR:

- Apparel
- Shoes
- Socks
- Sports Bag
- Protective Gear
- Transitional Clothing/Footwear

Special Notes: Include size

INTIMATE APPAREL:

- Bra
- Underwear
- Negligee
- Pajamas
- Gown
- Housecoat/Robe
- Slippers
- Housesocks (special socks with rubber sections on the bottom)

Special Notes: Include all necessary sizes

Jewelry:

- Ring
- Earrings – pierced or clip-on
- Necklace – preferred length
- Bracelet
- Charms
- Anklet – length
- Toe Ring
- Body Jewelry
- Watch – colored band or gold/silver, casual or fancy/dressy

Special Notes:

Bath/Body stuff:

- Body Moisturizers - lotion, cream, butter
- Fragrances – favorite brand, desired potency (cologne, eau de toilette, etc.)
- Bath Salts
- Shower Gel
- Body Scrub – favorite brand/scent, level of exfoliate
- Perfumed Drawer Liners – favorite scent

Special Notes:

Handbags:

Your favorite type/brand, length of strap, design/color or neutral

Special Notes:

Other Personal Items:

- Makeup – mascara, foundation, eye shadows, eye liners, blush, lip colors (list favorite brand)
- Nail polish – favorite brand/colors
- Hair Accessories
- Hosiery
- Beauty Application Tools – nail kit, makeup application brushes
- Belt – leather or not, width, size
- Luggage - leather or cloth, color, print/solid, size

Special Notes:

Reading Material:

- Books – genre, hardcover or paperback
- Magazines – favorites, one-time only or subscription

Special Notes:

ENTERTAINMENT:
- Movies – favorite genre or actor
- Music – favorite band, CD or MP3
- Live Performance – concert, musical, play, ballet, symphony, opera

Special Notes:

ANIMALS/PETS:
Specific parameters necessary

Special Notes:

HOBBIES:
- Supplies or Tools
- Class Time

Special Notes:

MISCELLANEOUS:

- Sunglasses
- Wallet – size, color, leather or cloth
- Key Ring
- Stationery – monogrammed, color, size
- Travel or Cosmetics Bag
- Umbrella
- Photo Frames – traditional or digital, size, wood, glass, trendy

Special Notes:

SPECIALTY:

- Engraved Gifts
- Cause-Related Gifts
- Knickknacks – type, brand, for specific room of the house
- Paraphernalia from Favorite Movie or TV Program

Special Notes:

Gift cards:

- Favorite Stores/Eateries

Special Notes:

Taboo Gifts:

List anything here you'd rather not receive as a gift at this time

Special Notes:

INTRINSICALLY VALUED GIFTS:

List anything here you'd like him to know you are interested in -- serving the community together, donating to a specific cause, etc.

Special Notes:

(Note to women: Keep this list updated at all times. Your honey won't necessarily need the whole list every time he goes out shopping but be sure he has enough information and your current wish list to make it easy for him. Give lots of detail – size, color, brand, best store to find the item, etc., so that he'll feel armed and ready to be successful.)

www.ingramcontent.com/pod-product-compliance
Lightning Source LLC
Chambersburg PA
CBHW031252280526
45784CB00004B/1816